Dear Ms. Wice,

Keep the torch lit! Your efforts are very much appreciated.

Sincerely,
O. McBride-Ahebee

Assuming Voices

By

Octavia McBride-Ahébée

Assuming Voices

Editorial material copyright ©2003 by Octavia McBride-Ahébée All rights reserved. No part of this book may be used or reproduced in any manner whatsoever without written permission except in the case of brief quotations embodied in critical articles and reviews. For information:

Lit Pot Press, Inc ,
3909 Reche Road, Ste. #132,
Fallbrook, CA 92028.

Cover design by Glenn A. Osborn © 2003

First U.S. Edition
Published by Lit Pot Press, Inc., Fallbrook, CA. USA
Printed in Canada by Stride Print Services

Library of Congress Cataloging in Publication Data

McBride-Ahébée, Octavia.
    Assuming Voices - First Edition 2003

1 Poetry
Library of Congress Control Number 2003112627
ISBN 0-9743919-1-3

Octavia McBride-Ahébée is a writer of poetry, short stories and plays. She is a Philadelphia native, who had lived in Cote d'Ivoire, West Africa for nine years. She is the mother of two children, Sojourner and Auguste, and a teacher to many.

This book is for
Auguste Seraphin Kouame Kouassi Ahébée;
mon coeur.

ACKNOWLEDGMENTS

Grateful acknowledgment is made to the following publications where several of these poems first appeared.

The Death of an Exile, Chas. M. Henry Printing Co., 1987.
Old Pictures and Black Walls, The Eagle Spirit, People's Voice Press, 1993.
Iron Market, International Quarterly, The Faces of the Americas, Vol.1, No. 4, 1994.
Against Myself, The Beloit Poetry Journal, Vol. 46, No. 4, Summer 1996

Table of Contents

Auguste *9*

Against Myself *11*

Iron Market *13*

The Sweetness of Pineapples *15*

In Defense of Flowers *19*

A Promise *21*

Homesick Spirits *23*

The Japanese Teahouse *25*

Round and Whole *27*

The Welcome *29*

No Home Here *35*

Lessons Unlearned *37*

The Flower of the Calabash *39*

Old Pictures and Black Walls......... *41*

The Death of an Exile *43*

Oasis......... *45*

A New Year's Greeting......... *51*

Jumping Into Memory......... *53*

Auguste

1.

It is your spirit they seek to exorcise,
to push with thin prayers and secret, celebratory praises
from our house
where we had planted flowers of protection.

Jump inside of me,
away from the swinging incense
and gutted chants
meant to trap and strip your retreating soul.

 I will take you for a dance
across the very floors where we made life,
Barron's *Sunshower* will frame your requiem,
and restore your faith.

2.

I am glad you are home with me,
in a house where love has always reigned,
running the hallways I had run,
racing to be a man for me.

You will grow, again,
to shed the weight of dead conventions,
to repeal pledges made to voles and vamps,
to become not my groom, again,
but our son.

3.

What pushed you to jump realms,
to leap across what we were living,
to even plan under the star that brought me to you,
for your departure,
for the hole in my heart,
for the one in your head?

4.
I sleep now,
in a sitting position,
my eyes pulled wide open
by pills I pop in neat intervals
to regulate my sadness,
while I wait to catch you
swinging on the arc of a night rainbow .

I swing on my father's redbrick terrace,
the one that is not covered—open to the elements,
I swing not back and forth in a rhythm that calms,
but side to side,
in a motion meant to evoke the spirits,
to wake the dead,
to push you from your hiding place
so I can say goodbye.

§ § §

Against Myself

she would part my hair in rhythms
using the pointed tips of grass
sharpened with her own teeth
making my scalp a canvas of walking patterns
with roped braids
standing only to be seen and glorified

carrying the deftness of the puppet master's mystery
her fingers-
when they still gave form to her hands-
kept the promise to hold my ease

but then the braids would loose their ropes
my reason would follow the moon

covered in the heads of corn flowers
in limbs of uprooted lemon grass
her eyes pushed closed from the weight of sunbeams
screamed *we had been girls together*
while I sung and swung amid the red hibiscus
hacking my friend whose belly was rounding itself with joy
whose fingers had not touched me at all

"Jesus!"

she pleaded with the calm of the spirit-filled
for Jesus.

§ § §

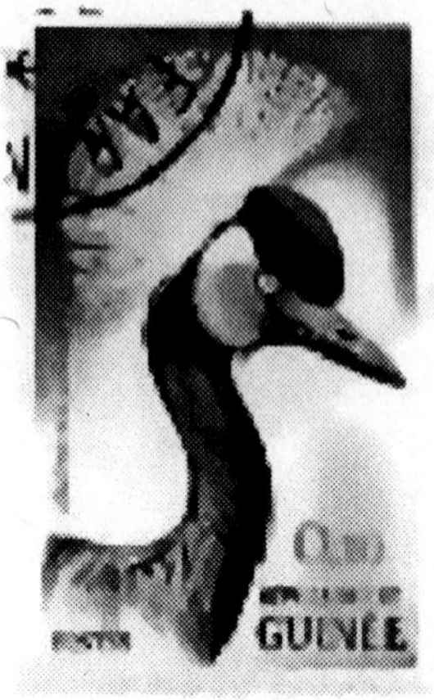
GUINEE

Iron Market

Desiré arrives home
right before the moon falls into La Gonave
and the sun, coy, smelling of human waste,
ascends from its night visit into Port-au-Prince.

During these dawn raids into our home,
Desiré, my bon mari, is always drunk on bark beer
consumed not in a whole evening of empty revelry
but from a moment, maybe a few,
after he has bent his knees,
knotted with the strength of bamboo sticks,
and opened his behind with the stoic arrogance
of a peacock spreading its plume,
to let in strangers from the North
for a gourde or two
to feed our stomachs
and bring color back to the hair of our children.

§ § §

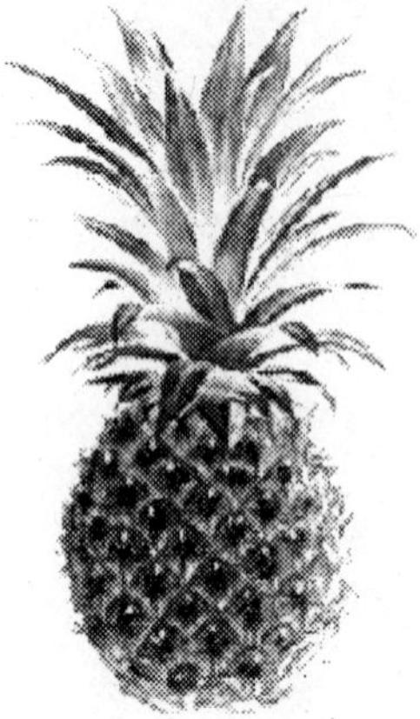

The Sweetness of Pineapples

1.
my son has the height of two machete blades
standing on the head of the other
this journey of hurried evil
of simple colonial play
will castrate his rise
he will not climb with boyhood insistence
even to the stature
of a stalk of standing corn

2.
our son kicks the small head of a child
now but a roving skull
freed from breathing skin
a football pushed through the hanging air
by the shoeless toes of its peers
children carrying cholera and machete wounds
as they strike to make a goal

3.
Hyacinth, a man fat with kindness and flesh
whose ears I used to taste with laughter
after listening to the voices of his body
wrestle with mine and the heat
and the dry hum of deaf bees,
is not in this camp of ghosts and demons and wingless locusts
to catch this soaring, tender head of bone
and give it peace
beneath our prostrated failure

4.
We are two now
me and my body
I am not bewitched
by the trailing maggots
the feces of my body's fear
restlessly haunting my womb
while still in search of new haunts
to celebrate this exodus
I crave only for the sight of a pineapple ring
buried in shards of carrots
and dry raisins from Belgium or France
the chance, again, to pull chest hairs
from Hyacinth's breasts as bloated as my own

5.
I am moved by the willfulness of my body
to vainly persist
though pilfered by the passions of ethnic fear
I, the child who thought the fur of mangoes was her own skin,
am now a mother who is ungenerous with her deserting
thoughts
dreaming only of the sweetness of pineapples colored with
carrots

6.
It is his habit, now, my boy, to battle
with familiar, belligerent ease,
wielding fingers with no roofs,
facing maggots, legless and marching,
a boy and a band worms
vying for milk, soured and littered,

left behind by a little girl
who is perhaps sucking the sky

7.
I tell the boy through the chatter of death rattles
against the blaring hush of the living
to unbound his kidneys
map a ring of urine lined with the salt of dead rain
made in the shape of a crucifix
to gird my body
to shield it
against the cravings of animals and non-believers
so I can go in peace.

§ § §

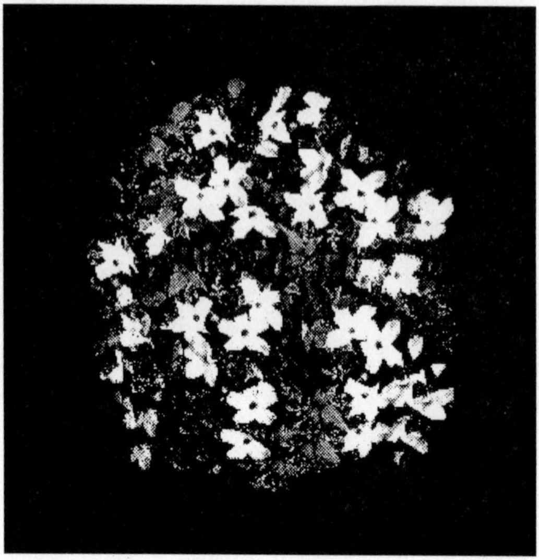

In Defense of Flowers

When I smell the wind of an Ak-47
before it sounds its name
before it travels in rounds of seconds
splintering the thoughts of sterile termites
pushing through the density of evil
in search of me

I run to hide in the voluminous fury of a jasmine shrub in
bloom
its pale butter blossoms shield me
from the bloodletting
bathing its roots

I snort, in silent gulps, which claim my dignity
the calming splendor of the jasmine's bouquet

I am rescued
for an instance
from a hunter high
on the dizziness of his own deprivation

I am rescued
from my brother
by a perfumed bush

§ § §

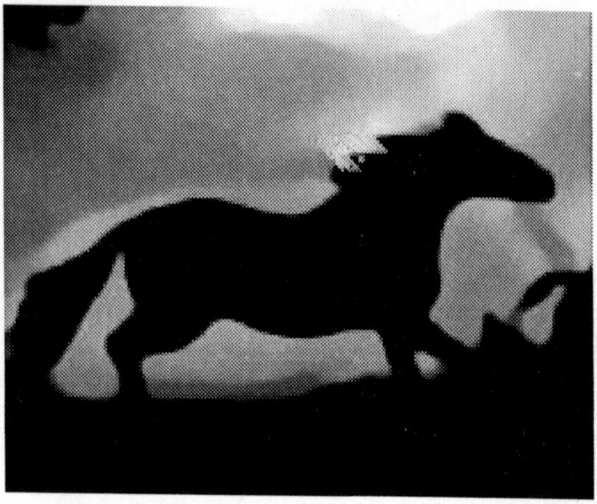

A Promise

He is an acrobat from Battambang
agile with ancient ways to share
who wears his hair as a horse's mane
-unbridled and always running-
His body swings in guises of suspension
flying with a hundred eyes
silencing natural spirits
inciting a riot to shock
a hunger for the base
for the fire of the inflamed spider monkeys
an appetite to spin a web of leaves into his head
He rebukes me
when I climb him through the duskiness to reach my own need
after the sun has suffocated itself
and I ride his back with the vengeance of angels
swollen by a promise
the spread of his toes heralds
holding on to his hair
the deceiving color of garden snails in heat
propelled by its dampness
its sweating limpness,
its sour scent of night
pained by its power to resist the seduction of my pull
He forces my dismount
flips me on my back
I see his lazy eye
alighted by the eyes of a jack-o-lantern
in wait
flushed
announcing his need to expel

He wants to tell me with words
about Cambodia
about children whose eyes are holding up the earth
women with cheeks and nipples the color of ox blood
old men who sweep rivers into sunsets
that drown your sight for fun
but we share no language of words
Let me sing to you, I say,
with the tips of my fingers
and I will find your words
during afternoon naps
when I can ride your back with clarity
rise to sleep in your aroma
luminous in its strength like your hair.

§ § §

Homesick Spirits

    Aya brought back,
carrying vestiges of her pride in her hip,
        a caged bird from the city
              whose tongue had been eaten
                  by the whipping tongues of red-headed salamanders
and whose throat, tautly strapped in a malachite choker
                with gems made of coffee and bark,
                    danced holding the cadence of lost crickets.

Aya, our village healer,
                              the child who pushed
                        feet first into an empty Friday
afternoon
            had grown flat, faithless in the knowledge
of her plants
in their power to seduce with fragrance and fear
these new homesick spirits
                    who stand at the doors of our breasts
        bu   ld
          i
                  ing tunnels with its anger to the tips
where our children once sucked relief
        from the taunts of companion spirits who float alone.

        I tore-off the dry reeds of my roof
cutting it with a dead cross
dressed in tired, singing cowry shells
            to let in the weight and tales of the rain
waiting beneath the stomach of a headless pain
        to offer my breast to a star in wanderlust

        after I had c l   awe
                            d
        the earth with the whole
of my body
            tempting it with the blood of dense life
if it would feast on the whole of my left dreams

        But Aya, my friend with two daughters

who lay in the ground with faces down,
                              hooded in dyed Guinea cloth
            with one breast between them,
                        said be p a t i e n t,
homesick spirits, she recently learned,
preferred to feed on the sorrow of silenced birds
              than   r
                      o
                          t   inside an aged breast

                  that

hangs   w   th   no
                i
                                           JOY.

                        § § §

The Japanese Teahouse

To Greg Witcher

I can now see
the skirt hems of hants
stitched by the hands of the living
they keep with them in this sphere
the shame and vanity of us all
and so hide their naked spirits
in calico gowns shielding indigo slips
made loose for easy movement

La Fleur cannot see the ghosts of this house
vying for perfume and overripe papaya
spreading like yeast
in anticipation of bounty
spreading with the unyielding spell of raw cauliflower
He hears their whispers
entangled in the whistling overtones of searching mice
their frosted threats to lick
the healing fungus off the backs of caterpillars
and press into dust with their weightless humor
another cloak of his torment
-the anointed AZT-

Yet his third eye is sane, blighted
perceiving the lust of fear
flapping in its own daydreams
anxious to walk backwards
with those who die away from home

La Fleur wants to sleep with cannons
near the vacant majesty of the Citadelle
under the guard of the grand Baron Samedi
in a grave that slides with no conscience
when the soil breathes too heavily
when forgotten things are collected
He wants to leave my city of foot-long sandwiches
and soft pretzels,
of trolley cars that triumph underneath the unbecoming frailty
of a cowed city
whose river has no bend
to return to Cap-Haitian
saluting the honeyed fantasies of home
spawned by the simple need
of man who can't build on the cunning of tomorrow

I whisper in his ear still open to thought
I hold his hand, scaled and aloof,
still greedy for the soles of other's fingertips
I say forget the cannons
and the piece of earth that exhales with no attention
my hants are vain
they dress in slips of purple and blue
today, we will sip evergreen plants
in the park where the Japanese teahouse sings
and we will berate any presumption
yours were days unspent.

§ § §

Round and Whole

Empty mango trees, drained of leaves and living color
hold only vultures,
the lone and last witness that I once was,
positioned in a congenital though merciful conspiracy
they look down on me
I stare up at their glorious, black, feathered cloaks
covering the skeletal, witless arms of this giant, sun-beaten,
fruit flower
these buzzards, angry at their own nature,
are compelled to banquet on my flesh
their hearts, they convey through their florid heads, bobbing
will not eat my soul as an appetizer
while my body rots on the side of the road
alone, except for the sole companionship
of someone's silent , crawling child,
dragging its limbs, disrupting dead memories
of thin, twisted strips of black licorice
eaten in times of plenty
a child, drained too, like the mango trees
but forever green
pulling with its neglected mouth at my left breast
spotted like a leopard, deflated like bagpipes
without the breath of a musician to give them context
                                        Empty

Full was once my life
but fullness-round and whole
light with ordinary innocence
like soap bubbles blown
from a child's unworldly mouth-
defies, distorts, disturbs your image of me

the African
I am a Dinka girl, complex
piled high like an anthill
I am a Dinka girl from Juba
black like the tar you pour on roads
to ease your travels and I am just as long
but I cover myself, on joyous journeys,
in cattle dung and red ocher for reasons you refuse to hold
I work hard, dance easily and suck the juice from mangoes
with a passion you will never touch
I make love in the open fields
when the sun has knocked down its glass walls
and only the cows and the moon's light are watching
and God tickling me with her approval
                              Full

I am one piece of a gaunt, faceless mass
to you
-a bloated stomach
emptied by inept, home-grown madmen-

We are stranded starfish spewed from the ocean
once part of something round and whole
now left on the road to rot
but, no, I am not alone on the shoulder of this road
here is a dying child and a horde of vultures
who will take me from you
and I will float in a generous atmosphere
wear an amulet around my neck to keep you out
eat stars when I am hungry
and still make love by the moon's light.

§ § §

The Welcome

Behind the back of fire
he pulled my fat plait and said the end of it
reminded him of a buffalo's tail,
coarse and resilient.

He asked in English that turned rough somersaults
if ever I rode a water buffalo
in a rice field
on the breath of water lilies
and felt I was riding on the shoulders of the sky.

I replied in English, harnessed and disciplined,
absent of rhythm
sterile as the standard is suppose to be
that this is America
I ride only cars and Moon's cousin, Jupiter,
the only course I want
is three chicken wings,
feathered with its limbs unfastened.

He smiled
unveiling a mouth left barren by cane and neglect
full of russets meshed with cinnabars and silent pinks
the colors of a Haitian rainbow after a blood storm.

The uneven stretches-fallen stories-
standing between his surviving teeth
softened me
opened me to question
where were the wrought-iron bars
shaped like tic-tac-toe boards

to block the hate and cage him in
allowing him to suffocate in peace
away from his fears of people
just afraid as he.

He said bars would block his reach for me
His chance to pull my plait and think of home.

"Hot sauce?" he asked. "Home?" I countered,
wondering if some woman took small happiness
from the deep-set wave of his lashes,

knowing that the storm outside
would catch a ride in the hub of my own.

This hoagie and rice bistro,
Asian-American food palace,
number playing pocket
where brown people full of blue defeats
dwarfed by a hunger to fly
place food orders, play numbers
and empty their impotence
in muted colors of screaming letters
scrawled on walls
proclaiming no room at the inn
for the yellow peril.

Home is Vietnam, he sung like a carol,
against the background bawling of an angry shower
whose pangs drowned even the calm of the 34 trolley
sweeping the avenue.

He then reached from his cage without bars
and touched the bridge of my nose,

pulling his sweaty finger
smelling of salt, swollen by hot grease,
down to the tip of it
and declared there were mountains he sat on at home
where young girls finger-brushed his lashes,
whispered with no sound what the moon and Jupiter knew,
mountains that were as strong and familiar as my nose.

My nostrils, his eyes remembered,
were as wide as welcoming as the holes he hid in
during moments that lasted forever
when the only feeling he heard
was the feces warming his legs
ranting he was still here under a hunchback sky.

Yes, I wanted hot sauce, I said,
transfixed like a deer
whose bowels are frozen by beams of light,
happy and empowered in the knowledge
I carried his home on my face.

The rain, alone, in its rancor running wild,
called out my home,
humming a small refrain of Haiti's wicked season
with its strength to strangle wails in its thunder,
swallow whole the orgasmic pleas of peasants,
wash butchered bodies of their blood
while pushing the buried to another stomping ground
after entering into a bond with the hills
to color them a lusty green
trimmed in the illusion of life in bloom.

I fled home in the night
in a pink dress patterned with rainbows
smelling of moth balls

a gift given to me by a man from America
who looked liked Jesus
and said the acid from grapefruits
left in a cat's molded urine
would erode the enmity
of the gonorrhea
eating my stomach with an unquenchable rage,
another gift from the generous man from the North
who came South to save souls
but laid his own seeds.

I fled home with 42 bodies of hope
in a boat built with none
a boat unfamiliar with the magnitude of sustained desire
spooked by the weighty fears
of those riding in it
and the moon's promise of crazed retribution
if it failed to move to the cruel rhythm of the lunar beat.

We held on with our dread and our vomit
and the death grips they gave
when we thought of home
and heads of lovers
-faces full of lashes and hyssop-stained breath-
without bodies
that rolled
with no wind behind them
down hills that hollered even when the sun was hanging.

I kept my eyes opened but rolled back
to lay no claim as a witness for the curious
of the fortunate who fell into the rough mercy
of a disinterested sea
my frigid body

numbed by the phlegm of waves of happy agony
remained inflamed by the fervent groping
of bodies still claiming allegiance to hope
begging me not to bury them
by my inaction
in a grave full of salt
a grave that would eat their eyes away.

I have eaten my faith of finding small happiness
in the depth of a curl of a lash
of waking on the tail of a night
smelling hyssop, wanted breast milk,
lover's putty
-not sensing only the absence of things-
I have eaten such faith and survived
like Trinh's teeth,
rotten and still under a hunchback sky.

I now turn somersaults in the land of Yankee kings
never landing with the indelicate grace of Trinh's husky lilt
I am the custodian of whims
imagined only in the minds of jilted demons
overindulged and empty
ever eager to ask in the temper of the unloved
Where is your green-card ?

I mourn during sun showers,
when I am riding some woman's child on my shoulders
imploring them to imagine
they are riding on the shoulders of the sky,
for my boy whose mouth must be full of teeth now
whose face carries mine, but not my mouth prints
I mourn for the lost chance
when I could have fallen in a grave of salt,
had my eyes and hope eaten like a carnival feast.

My chicken wings are ready, he said,
and he brought them out
along with a brush,
the kind with hard, plastic bristles,
that makes furrows in your head
like a plow does a field.

He said he would sweep my hair of my longing
while I watched the rain
while we both thought of the homes still sitting with us.

As he undid my plait
and pulled the brush through my hair
his body's scent
as singular as the smell of death
and burning leaves and lovemaking
surrounded me and said welcome.

§ § §

No Home Here

Each blow, grounded and measured,
Each pounding seemingly incessant,
Of intractable yam
Debarked
Beaten into another life form
Following the orbit of forebears
Swelling the undemanding appetites of the easily sated
Stills the fire in my head
Trapping it in an open awareness that I am not home

I think of Phillis and am ashamed
I share her judgment of fated rescue.

§ § §

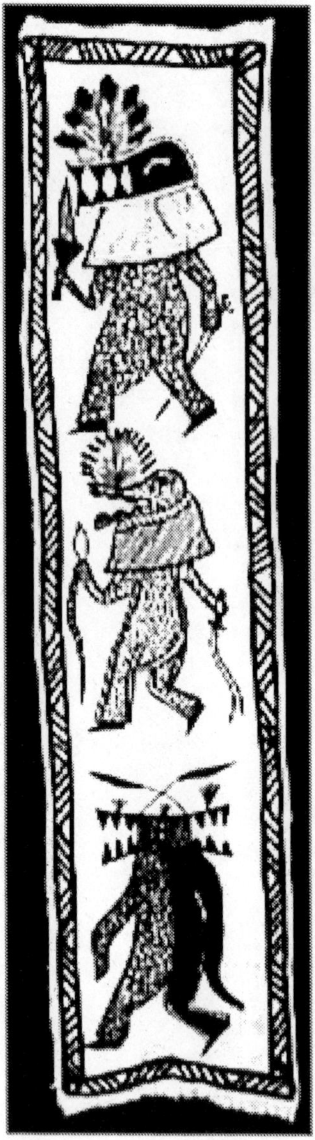

Lessons Unlearned

Three pass my face, feet
marching in blue rubber flops
shoes of soldier-boys.

Their toes but starved worms
picked raw by stiff rain, they seek
reprieve in bush hooch

Pecking machetes
hang from belts of spent palm leaves
hitting ankles numb.

Me, a Merico*
hiding on the back of dirt
bidding for the past.

§ § §

* Merico-descendants of African-Americans who repatriated to Liberia in the 1800s.

The Flower of the Calabash

I give you the curve of my back
contorted into C's shape
supported by herring rods and cut vertebrate
in the crowded marché
of masks and walking sticks
and in between my perusal of mud cloth and talking drums
I clearly hear the march of your tuna cans,
your prosthesis of thrown away tin,
your invention for moving through the world.

§ § §

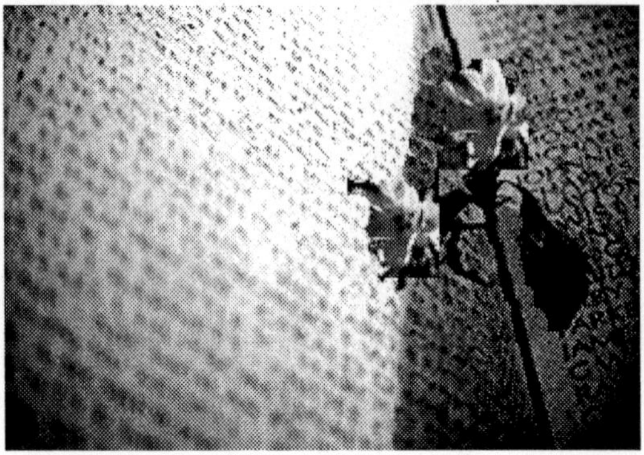

Old Pictures and Black Walls

Old pictures whisper through cracked
and faded ink,
through haze and lack of photographers' skill
of the lazy eye you carried,
cold and clear and lonely
-like a child's abandoned marble-
upon a face a blade had no need to tread.

It is the cherry blossom season,
the sun is standing high and hot,
the heat and fragrance rub against the other
trying to fool me into feeling
that the simple swinging scent
of a cherry blossom in flight
wrapped in the warmth of a benign ray
can forgive all that is ugly with its sweet self.

To think that we are same in age
you in death and me in life
with flat stomachs as hard as the head of a hammer,
with corned-covered feet as long and as well traveled
as Broad Street,
with fears as big and heavy as an African elephant
inspires simple yet frenzied fantasies
like me cupping in the palm of my hand
just for the hell of it
your high Cherokee cheekbone
or pressing my parted lips against it
and saying good day Daddy.

But I stand firm and full of fury
like the sun
before this great black wailing wall,
then I see the name that numbs me
~~~~~~~~~~~~~~~~~~~~~~~~-yours-
 I walk my knuckle in the
carved crevice of your name
thinking who but a generous mother
of yesteryear
would give such a gift as your name.

I took my thoughts and inhaled them
along with the scent of cherry blossoms and the heat.

§ § §

The Death of an Exile

In whose armpit will I bury my face, Brutus
and smell the scent of home

there in his excrement as eternal as the earth
he laid
shrouded in some sickly sorrow
romantic death kindly keeps to itself

what an anticlimax, Brutus
my heart was hot for more

the absence of blood brought no catharsis
no cascading conflagration
that could inflame his body and make it
convulse
name come alive and scream to itself

whose blistered hands will touch my body,
Brutus
and make me feel myself

our time together was throttled by transported
memories
of his forsaken home my mind never knew
circumstance had not meant us to calmly
complement the other
to fly to familial raptures as normal father
and child do

When I run along the Susquehanna
and wonder at its name

I will leap into the Limpopo, Brutus
and carry the pain of memory on my back.

§ § §

Oasis

***For Côte d'Ivoire
and the students of the
International Community School of Abidjan***

I come each day
to the whole of the world,
sometimes five minutes late,
often with Hoppe to unlock the door,
always a hoarse voice
seemingly squeezed barren
rises to salute me.
I hear through the boom of its *Good Morning*
Nigeria's will.

A face freckled with Norway pine
crisscrosses my movements
before I turn another lock
offering tidbits of U.S. presidential stats,
and as I mark our time in the world
with yellow dust on a forest-green board,
a beautifully wrapped Belgian,
encased in a hot pink hanbok,
doles Swiss chocolates
and insights from her father's Zaire.

I rest my Moroccan orange bag,
woven by dreamed-filled fingers
from Madagascar, on my desk,
a bag I carry with any color dress
because when I do

I feel the pull of an Ottawa spirit.

Inevitably, a New World face,
looking deceptively like India,
but belonging to bridges
that lead to everywhere
walks me back to Nairobi,
to medium-grilled zebra at Carnivore
and pushes me into Toronto,
his newest love,
where mice,
in the sanitized splendor of fast food,
serve treats of cheese.

I move forward, on my own,
into the inner circle
of my horseshoe
to view the whole beauty of the world.

Marble eyes,
like those I shot in childhood play,
whose color I must always ponder,
pierce me.
I feel the wisp of Virginia breezes
but just that,
when the voice of these eyes
dresses in her mother's voice
to preserve the River Thames.
I smile
and know that the hand of the wind
touches in different ways.

I turn forward
into the sands of the Sahara

propelled by the gentle flow of a river giving birth
in colors of blue and white,
a giant soul
contained in a small, starched boubou
offers a dessert,
an oreo cookie, a salted cracker,
the sage experience of familial spirits,
a show of how high
Arabic's lightening lilt
can jump and then sit down with grace.

And then my chi,
in the guise of a boy from Nimo
in whose heart runs green and white,
reasserts itself,
demanding with soccer's singular ardor
a current event,
a scheduled map test,
the promise to give him the world.

I turn, again,
chilled
by a fragile voice
bathed often in borscht
and breezes from Balkhash,
inviting a challenge,
in a whisper weltered in modesty
to find Almaty,
the apple place of her heart,
which lives between Atlanta and Abidjan.

A girl,
dressed in the shade of blue
mapmakers color the seas,
with a white star in her hair, and whose mouth is watered

by the Webi Shabelle,
a girl who hangs from a kapok tree
when she dreams of Juba and incense from home,
who blows a horn to call the world,
screams to the whisper
that she once danced in Kazakstan.

And then my craving heart,
wearing a tucked t-shirt and shorts
and shoes with laces untied
to pull the unwanted wonders of the world,
lifts a head
covered in kindness' smile
and framed in the colors of life
-dark and brown-
betraying his intent
to dance, too
but beneath the moon's glare
and point to his place in the world.

I pause for a moment,
to take hold of my blessings
when I am lulled
by the beat of God's bounty,
-small, soft and deep-
announcing the ways
in which she moves.
Not all can hear, but I do.
A mystery from Abuja,
shielded in the warmth
of what affirms,
the little girl artiste
who is able to walk through the façade
and render what is real.

Real like the monsoon
blown in from India by way of Korea,
landing on the coast of Ivory,
a dynamo buoyed by the prudence of yin/yang
but whose zeal is unleashed,
laying claim to all.
A girl storm with Seoul,
whose not afraid to open doors
even for ancestors
or walk through them
bearing gifts of kimbob and Vanessa Mae.

And my boy chiefs,
reigning from a coast
once breathing with gold
and from where air
kisses your face
with a slow, sweeping whisk,
read their legends
of ladybugs with dinosaur heads
and gorilla legs with knees
that protrude like omniscient binoculars,
throw me a glare
when I offer comment
on their literary appetites.

I have my chameleons
from Indiana plains
and California deserts
who blend their stars and stripes
to sing of Africa.

I have hope
who fills my doubts with new births,

a lion from Ambesili
who assails my gloom,
an elephant from Abidjan
who leaves his presence everywhere.

I come each day
to the whole of the world,
sometimes five minutes late,
but always with hope.

§ § §

A New Year's Greeting from Abidjan to Philly

We are the people, who fly,
searching for what was taken,
turning our ears to catch our mothers' rhyme.

At last we have landed,
in the garden of our fathers.
Thank you.
Thank you for your fat homilies filled with hants
who laid with us,
under the weight of story quilts,
never forgetting the rough passage
and the times when laughter was queen.

§ § §

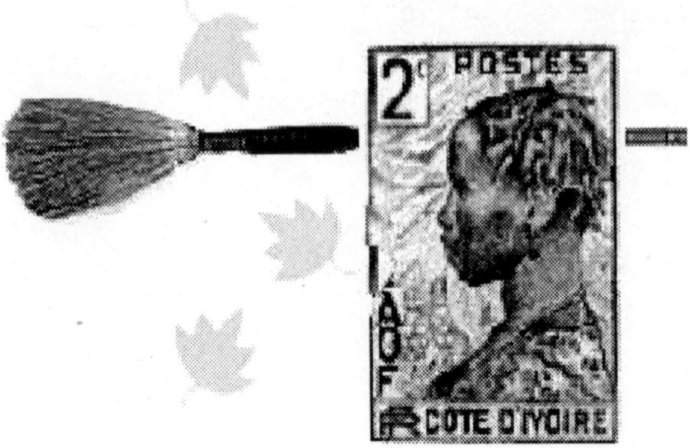
2c
POSTES
A O F
RF
COTE D'IVOIRE

Jumping Into Memory

A broom,
wearing the dust of the harmattan,
sits in its simple majesty
between two baby shoes,
Sojourner's and mine,
above the head of light,
her window.

A broom,
brash and impudent,
sweeping legal presumption
that we don't love
into a cloud masquerading as hope.
A broom,
brave enough to carry the weight of love.

A broom,
that lets new life begin
with one jump.

I got baby shoes,
one hunter green and one egg-shell white with opened toes,
standing like Behanzin's guardians
in a little girl's room in Abidjan
a little girl with memory to fill
a girl away from home and yet at home.

A broom.

I got a broom protecting the memories
and begging to tell of kinds of stories.

I got my broom.

§ § §